AUSTRALIAN LEADLIGHT DESIGNS

Jillian Sawyer

Kangaroo Press

Foreword

Leadlighting is becoming increasingly popular in Australia, particularly as a hobby. Unfortunately, most of the design books available are American in origin and not applicable to our unique Australian heritage.

The familiar cry from students in the craft is "Where can I get some truly Australian designs?"

So, for my students and hopefully, many others Australia wide, I have attempted in this book to capture in glass a selection of the wonderful abundance of colour and variety provided by our own Australian flora and fauna.

Where possible I have depicted the birds, animals and wildflowers as naturally as is possible, working within the restrictive boundaries of glass.

These designs are suited to both lead and copperfoil, though the more complicated (those with many small pieces) are better suited to the copperfoil procedure which, by its very nature, allows for much finer detail than lead.

To the beginner, remember, there is no such word as "can't" and with perseverence you can produce work which will both delight and satisfy you.

To the uninitiated, whose appetite may have been whetted by the designs in this book, I recommend you contact the stained glass studio nearest you, which holds courses in the art of leadlighting. Failing the availability of such a studio, I recommend the two most useful books I know:

For leadlighting procedures: *How to Work in Stained Glass* (Second Edition) by Anita & Seymour Isenberg.

For design procedures: *How to Design for Stained Glass (Even if you don't know how to draw)* by Kazanjian & Rosey.

Thanks to Wayne McOnie for photographic work—an excellent student who became a valued friend.

Also to Bert Lennerts of Design Glass—for his unfailing encouragement of this project.

Finally, I thank my husband—who pushed me when I needed pushing most. This book is for you, Brian.

Jillian Sawyer
Firebird Leadlights
1030 Albany Highway
East Victoria Park W.A. 6101

Reprinted 1990, 1991 and 1992
First published in 1987 by Kangaroo Press Pty Ltd
3 Whitehall Road (P.O. Box 75) Kenthurst 2156
Printed in Hong Kong by Colorcraft Ltd

ISBN 0 86417 166 8

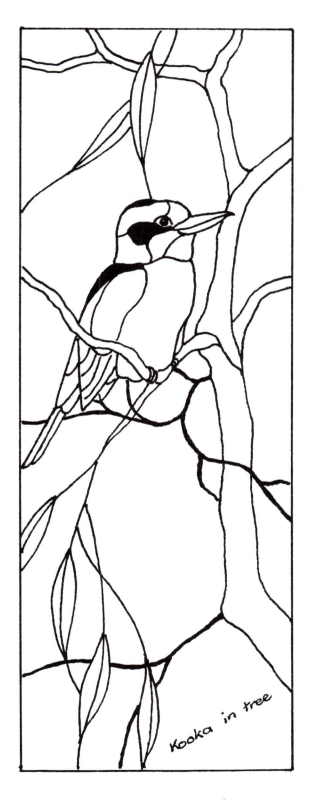

Kooka in tree

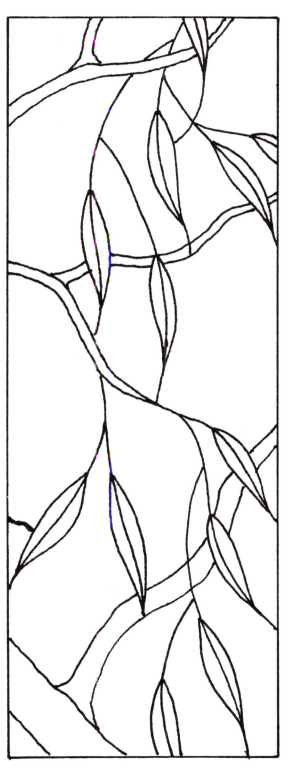

3

Sulpher Crested
Cockatoos
at Sunset

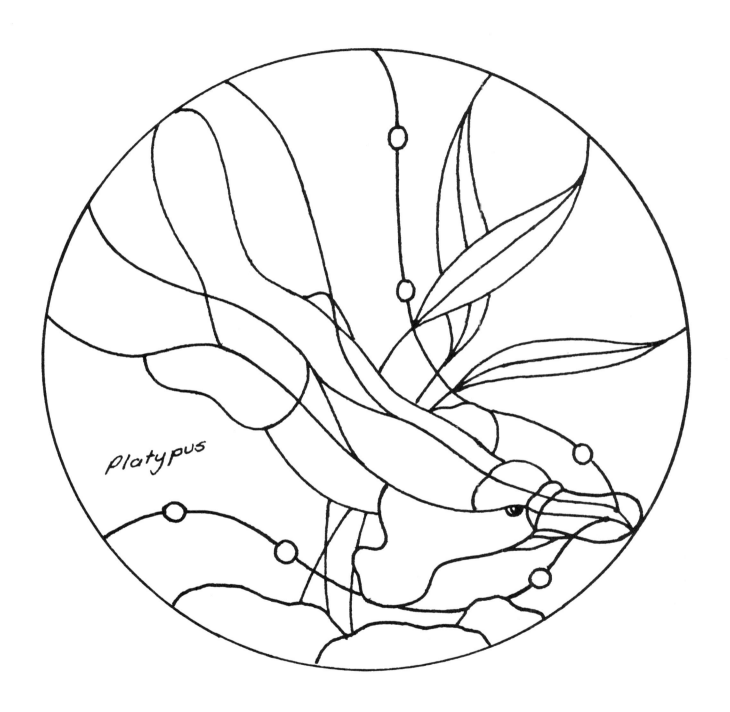

platypus

Rainbow
lorikeets

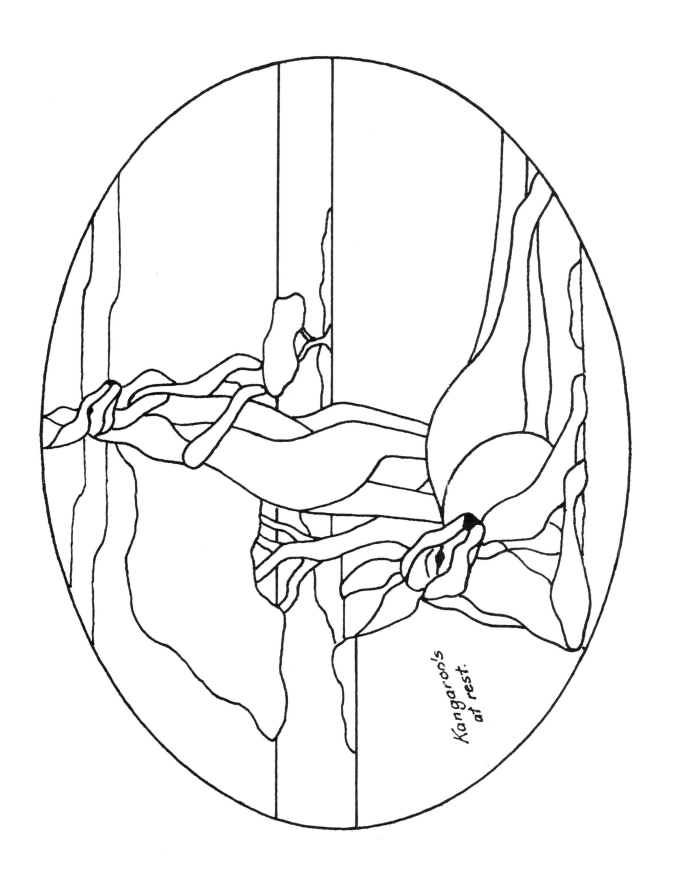

Kangaroo's at rest.

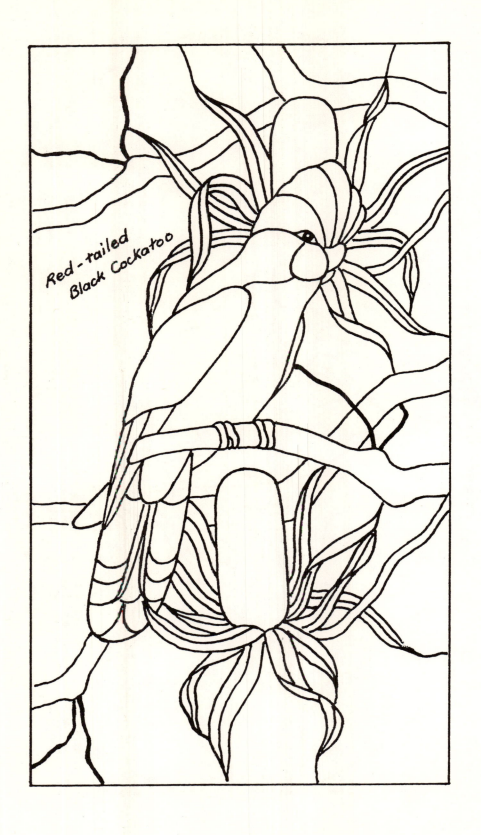

Red - tailed
Black Cockatoo

Black-shouldered
Kite

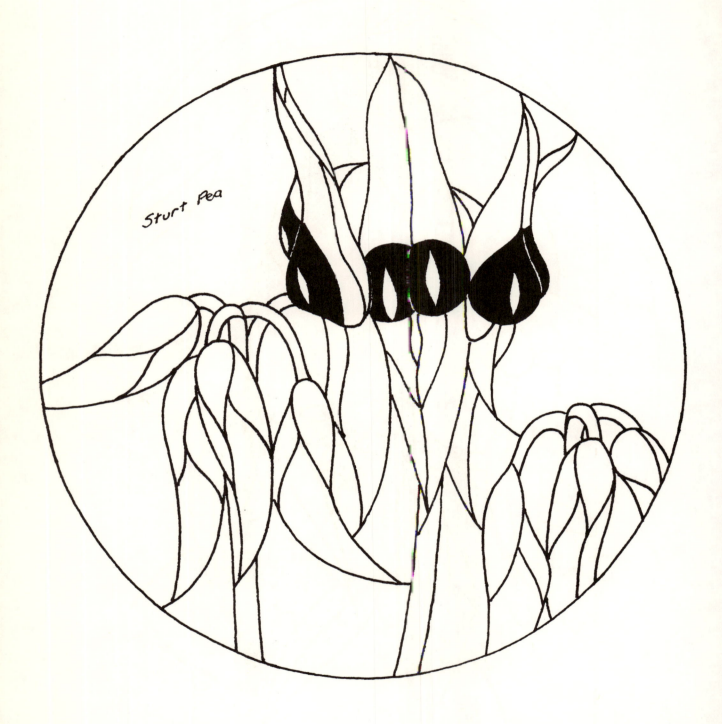

Sturt Pea

10

Gum-Nuts

Koalas

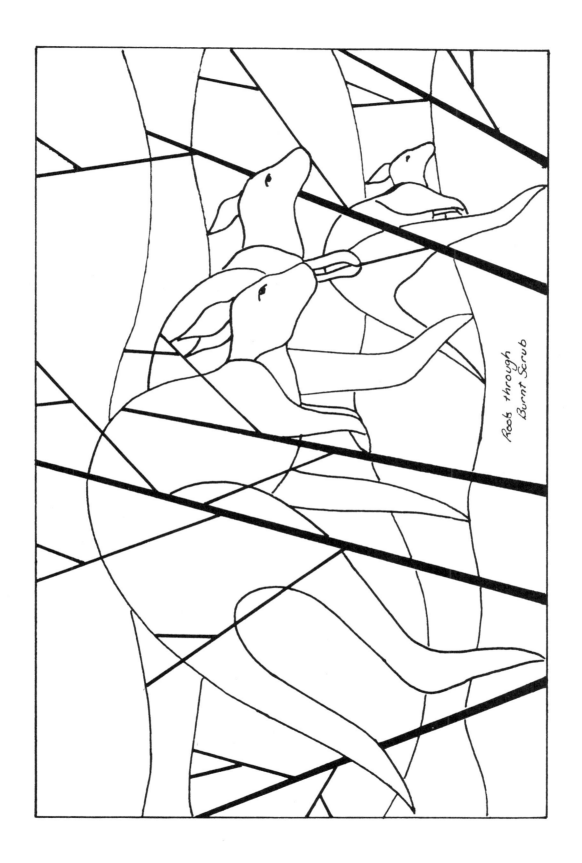

Roos through
Burnt Scrub

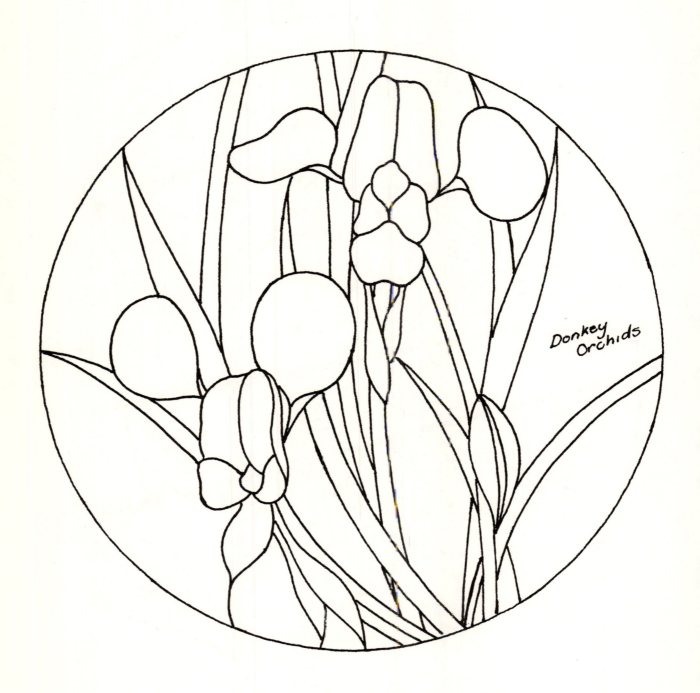

Donkey
Orchids

14

Sun Orchids

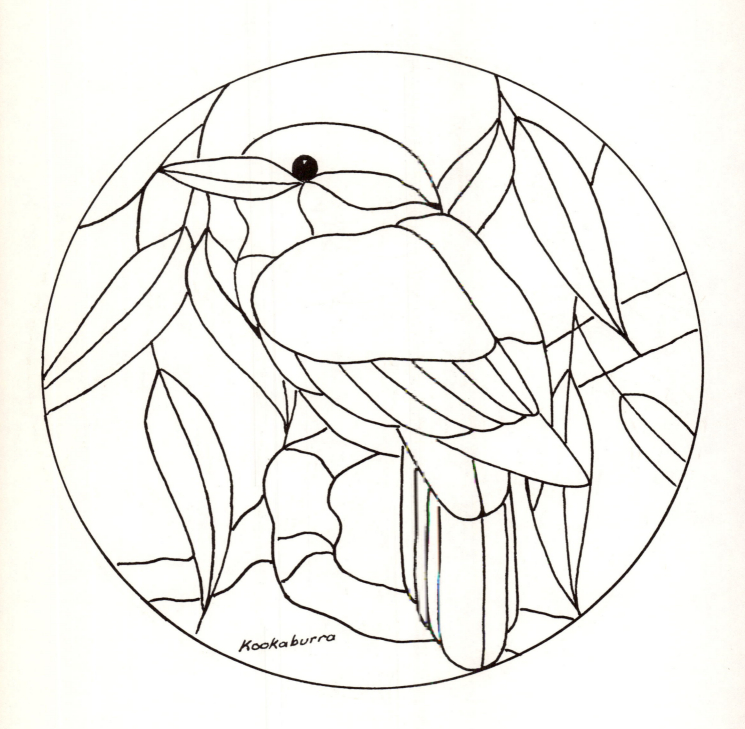

Kookaburra

16

Eastern
Rosella

Superb Blue Wren

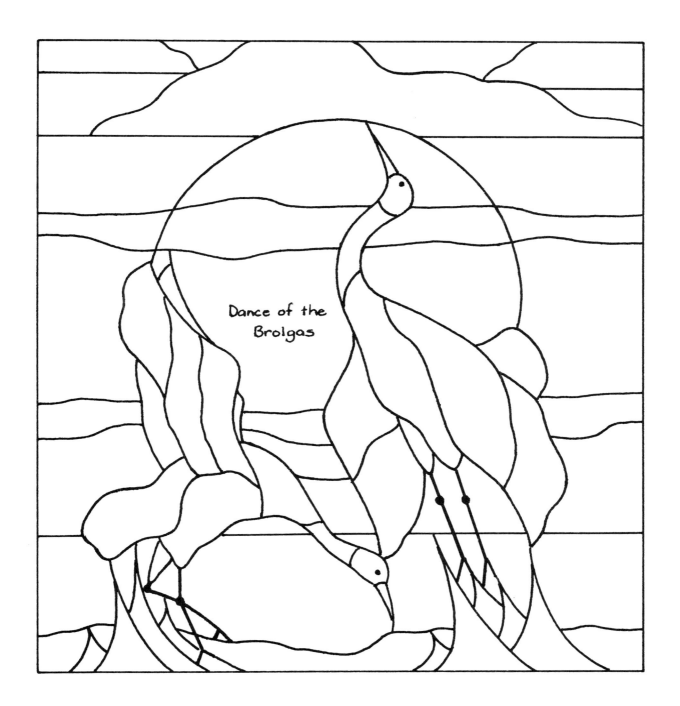

Dance of the
Brolgas

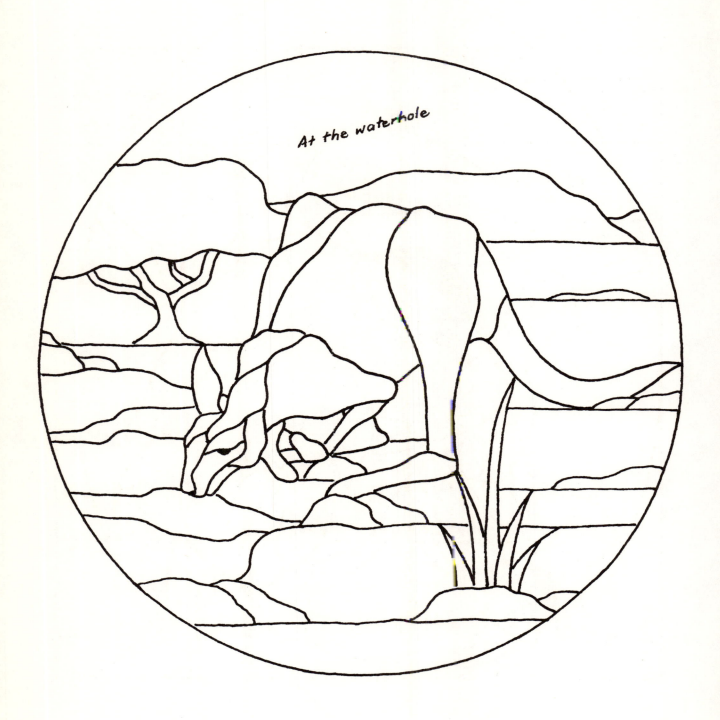

At the waterhole

20

Blue-winged
Kookaburra

Sugar Glider

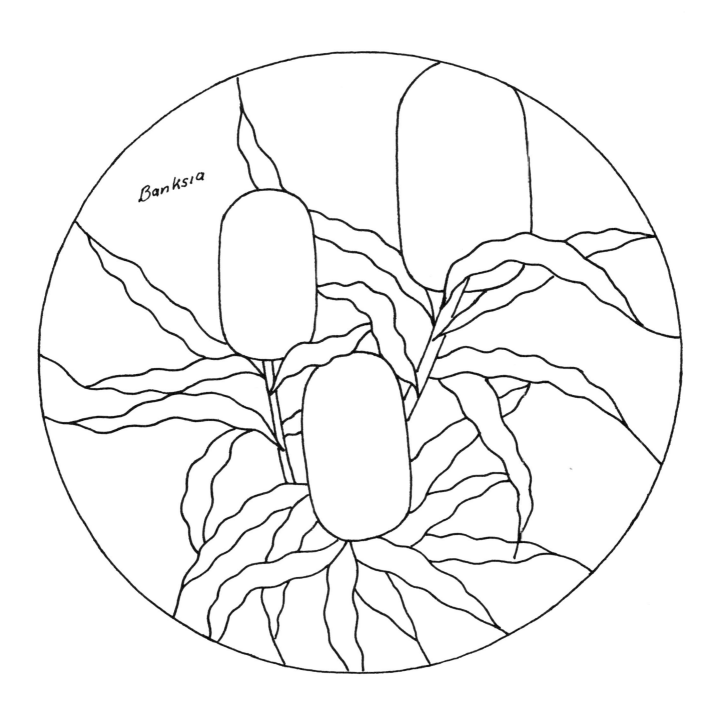

Banksia

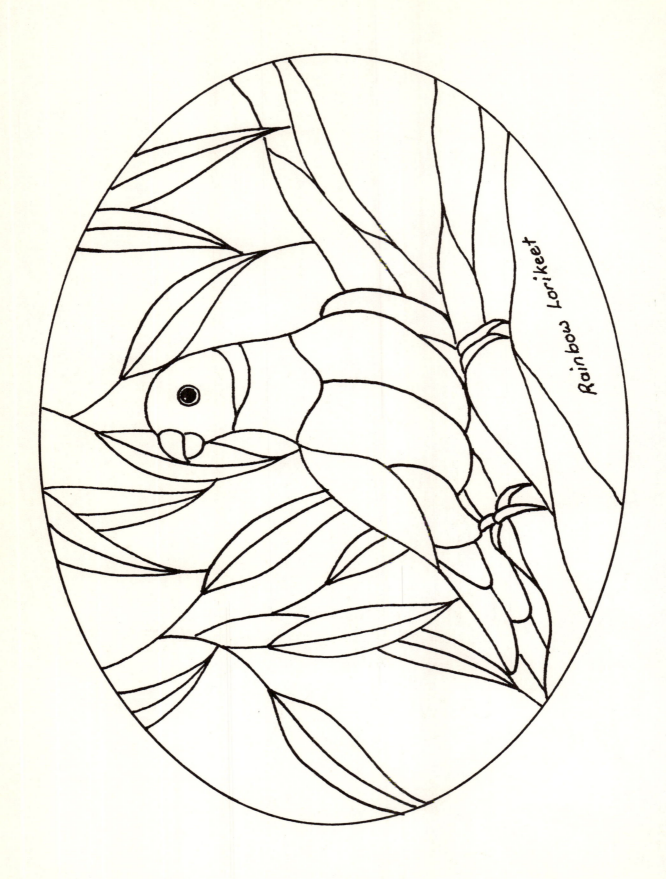

Rainbow Lorikeet

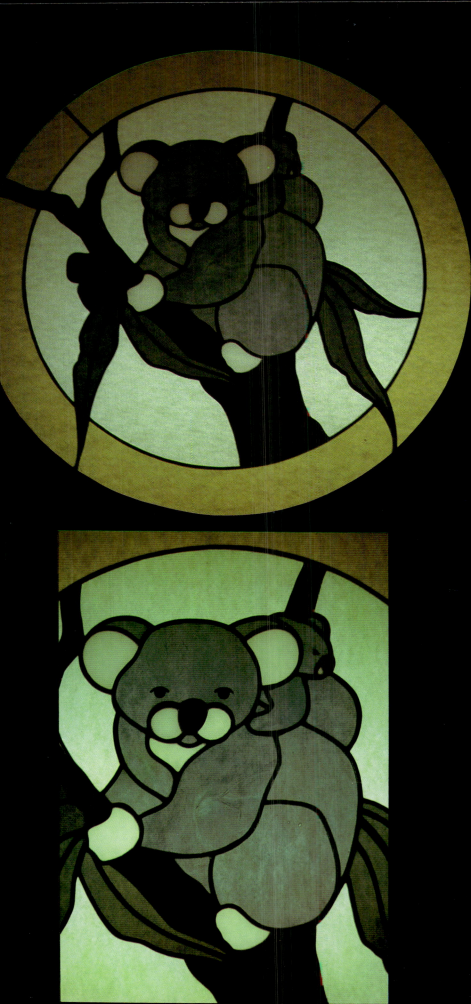

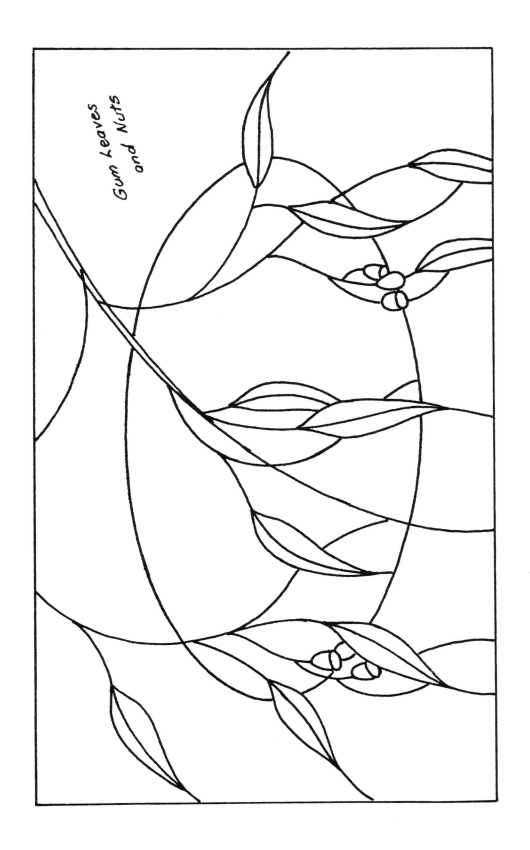

Gum Leaves and Nuts

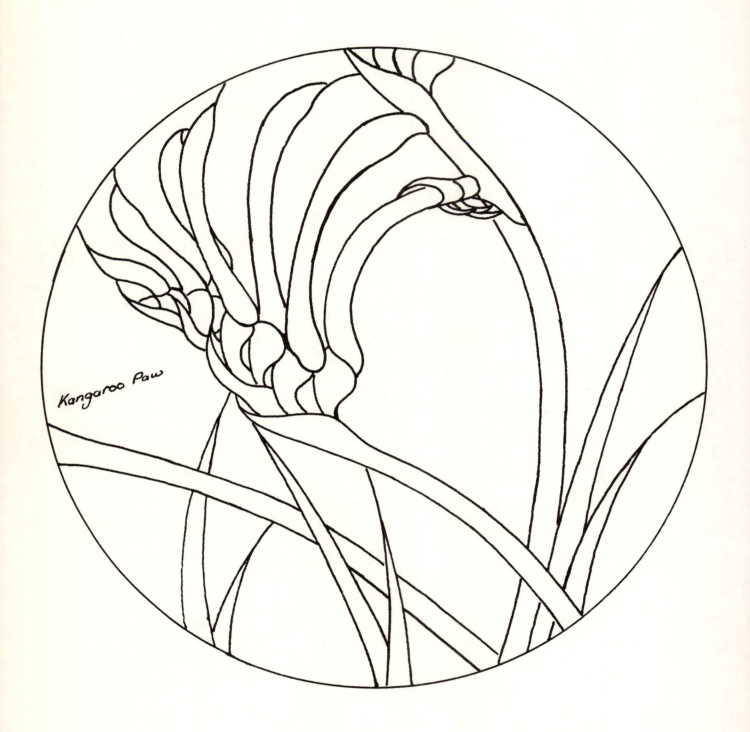

Kangaroo Paw

26

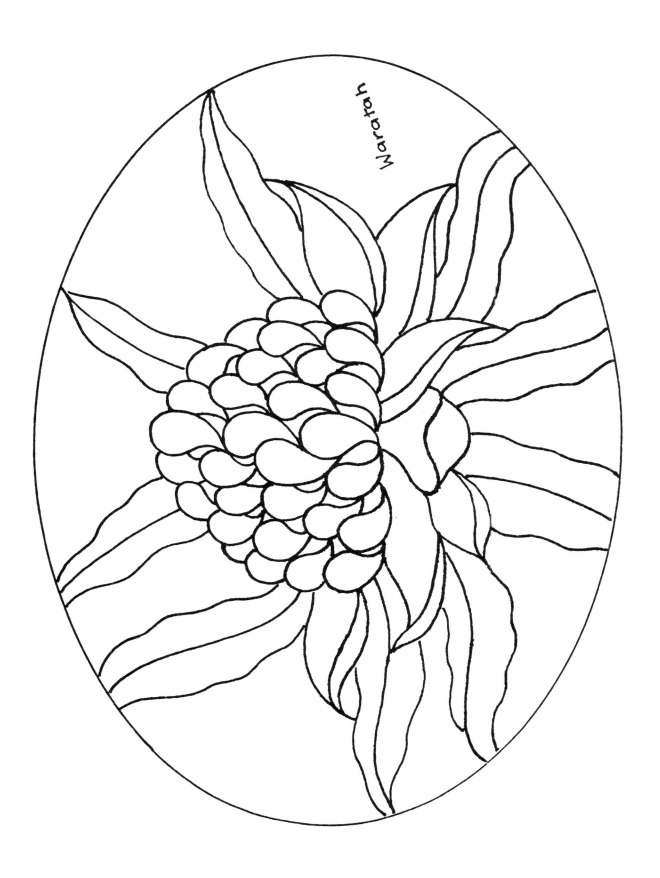

Gum Leaves

Major Mitchell
Cockatoo

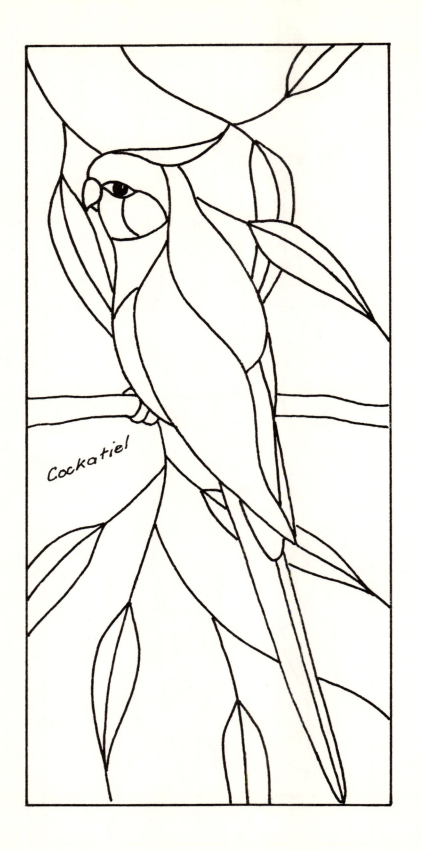

Cockatiel

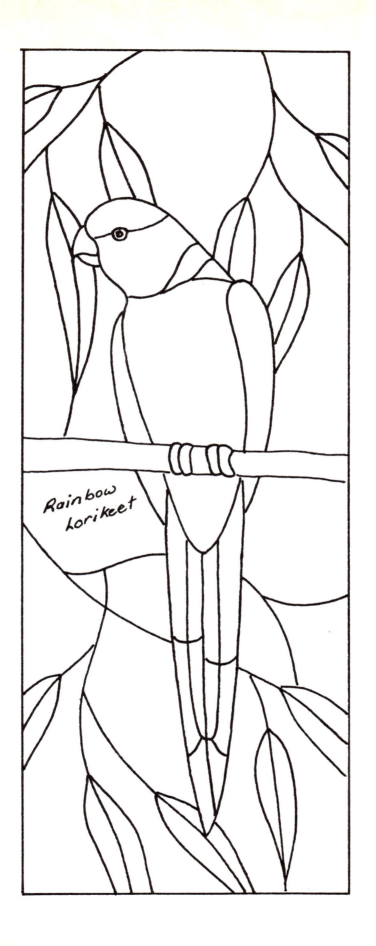

Rainbow
lorikeet

Eastern Rosella